Intelligence
Psychology

The complete explanations, definitions, theories, IQ levels, measurements & types of human intelligence

Reference

Dr. Christopher Robertson (November 2016) Intelligence Psychology. (Online) Available at: http://www.amazon.com (Accessed: 3rd September 2016).

About the Book

This is a book that has the complete information regarding the human intelligence Psychology in detail as under;

- o The introduction, explanation and definitions
- o The top theories presented by psychologists till date
- o The measurements of intelligence identification
- o The IQ tests and scorings
- o The nine specific types of human intelligence

This book strongly helps you understand the mentality and behaviors as well as the likes and dislikes of the people you have concerns in personal and social life.

This book also helps you to understand, to deal with or educate your children greatly as well as to understand the specific type of intelligence they are gifted from the God your Lord.

Teachers and parents must read and study this book closely to understand the intelligence type of their kids deeply.

Table of Contents

<u>**Intrapersonal Intelligence (Self Smart)**</u>

<u>**Spatial Intelligence (Picture Smart)**</u>

<u>**Existential Intelligence or spiritual intelligence**</u>

================================

Introduction to Intelligence

Human intelligence, mental quality that comprises of the capacities to learn from the matter of experience, adjust to new circumstances, comprehend and handle dynamic ideas, and utilize information to control one's surroundings.

A great part of the excitement among agents in the field of intelligence gets from their attempts to decide precisely what intelligence is. Distinctive examiners have stressed diverse parts of intelligence in their definitions. For instance, in a 1921 symposium the American psychologists Lewis M. Terman and Edward L. Thorndike contrasted over the meaning of intelligence,

Terman focusing on the capacity to think uniquely and Thorndike accentuating learning and the capacity to give great reactions to questions. More recently, however, psychologists have for the most part concurred that adjustment to nature is the way to comprehension both what intelligence is and what it does. Such adjustment may happen in an assortment of settings: an understudy in school takes in the material he needs to know keeping in mind the end goal to do well in a course; a physician treating a patient with new side effects finds out about the fundamental ailment; or a craftsman modifies an artistic creation to pass on a more intelligible impression. Generally, adjustment includes rolling out an improvement in oneself keeping in mind the end goal to adapt all the more viably to the earth, yet it can likewise mean changing nature or finding an altogether new one. Effective adjustment draws upon various intellectual procedures, for example, recognition, learning, memory, reasoning, and problem solving. The primary accentuation in a definition of intelligence, then, is that it is not a psychological or mental process in essence yet rather a particular blend of these procedures that is purposively coordinated toward compelling adjustment. In this manner, the physician who finds out about another ailment adjusts by seeing material on the illness in therapeutic writing, realizing what the material contains, recalling the significant angles that are expected to treat the patient, and afterward using motivation to take care of the issue of applying the data to the requirements of the patient. Intelligence, altogether, has come to be viewed not as a solitary capacity but rather as a powerful drawing together of numerous capacities. This has not generally been evident to agents of the subject, be that as it may; surely, a great part of the historical backdrop of the field rotates around arguments in regards to the nature and abilities that constitute intelligence.

Collective Definitions

In this segment we exhibit definitions that have been proposed by groups or organizations. By and large definitions of intelligence given in reference books have been either contributed by an individual psychologist or quote a prior definition given by an analyst. In these cases we have credited the quote to the psychologist, and have set it in the following area. In this area we just rundown those definitions that either can't be credited to a particular people, or speak to an aggregate definition settled upon by numerous people. The same numbers of word references source their definitions from different lexicons; we have attempted to dependably list the original source.

1. "The capacity to utilize memory, learning, knowledge, understanding, reasoning, creative ability and judgment keeping in mind the end goal to take care of issues and adjust to new circumstances." All Words Dictionary

2. "The ability to secure and apply knowledge." The American Heritage Dictionary, fourth release

3. "People contrast from each other in their capacity to comprehend complex thoughts, to adjust viably to nature, to gain as a matter of fact, to participate in different types of reasoning, to beat snags by taking thought." American Psychological Association

4. "The capacity to learn, comprehend and make judgments or have assessments that depend on reason" Cambridge Advance Learner's Dictionary

5. "Intelligence is an extremely broad mental capacity that, in addition to other things, includes the capacity to reason, arrange, take care of issues, think dynamically, grasp complex thoughts, take in rapidly and gain as a matter of fact." Common explanation with 52 expert signatories

6. "The ability to learn truths and aptitudes and apply them, particularly when this

capacity is exceptionally created." Encarta World English Dictionary

7. "ability to adjust adequately to the environment, either by rolling out an improvement in oneself or by changing the environment or finding another one intelligence is not a solitary mental process, but instead a blend of numerous mental procedures guided toward powerful adjustment to the environment."Encyclopedia Britannica

8. "the general mental ability required in calculating, reasoning, perceiving relationships and analogies, adapting rapidly, putting away and recovering data, utilizing dialect fluidly, arranging, summing up, and acclimating to new circumstances." Columbia Encyclopedia, 6th release

9. "Limit with regards to learning, reasoning, understanding, and comparable types of mental action; inclination in getting a handle on truths, connections, realities,

implications, and so forth." Random House Unabridged Dictionary

10. "The capacity to learn, comprehends, and contemplates things." Longman Dictionary or Contemporary English

11. "the capacity to learn or comprehend or to manage new or attempting circumstances the gifted utilization of reason (2): the capacity to apply information to control one's surroundings or to think dynamically as measured by target criteria (as tests)" Merriam-Webster Online Dictionary

12. "The capacity to procure and apply learning and aptitudes." Compact Oxford English Dictionary

13. "The capacity to adjust to the environment." World Book Encyclopedia

14. "Intelligence is a property of mind that envelops numerous related mental capacities, for example, the abilities to reason, arrange, take care of issues, think

uniquely, fathom thoughts and dialect, and learn." Wikipedia

15. "Limit of psyche, particularly to comprehend standards, truths, certainties or implications, get information, and apply it to hone; the capacity to learn and grasp." Dictionary

16. "The capacity to learn and comprehend or to manage issues." Word Central Student Dictionary

17. "The capacity to fathom; to comprehend and benefit from experience."WorldNet

18. "The ability to learn, reason, and get it." Words Myth Dictionary

Psychologist Definitions

This section contains definitions from psychologists. Now and again we have not yet figured out how to find the correct reference and would value any assistance in doing as such.

1. "Intelligence is not a solitary, unitary capacity, yet rather a composite of a few capacities. The term signifies that mix of capacities required for survival and headway inside a specific culture." A. Anastasias

2. "That aspect of mind basic our ability to think, to tackle novel issues, to reason and to know about the world." M. Anderson

3. "We can't help thinking that in intelligence there is a major workforce, the change or the absence of which, is absolutely critical for real world life. This personnel is judgment, generally called great sense, down to earth detect, activity, the workforce of adjusting ones self to conditions." A. Benet

4. "We might utilize the expression "intelligence" to mean the capacity of a living being to take care of new issues." W. V. Bingham

5. "Intelligence is what is measured by intelligence tests." E. Exhausting

6. "a quality that is scholarly and not passionate or moral: in measuring it we attempt to preclude the impacts of the youngster's energy, intrigue, industry, and so forth. Besides, it means a general limit, a limit that goes into everything the tyke says or does or considers; any need of "intelligence" will in this manner be uncovered to some degree in all that he attempts;"C. L. Burt

7. "A man has intelligence seeing that he has learned, or can learn, to conform himself to his surroundings." S. S. Colvin

8. "The ability to arrange and structure one's conduct with an end in view."J. P. Das

9. "The ability to learn or to benefit by experience." W. F. Dearborn

10. "In its most reduced terms intelligence is available where the individual creature, or person, knows, however faintly, of the significance of his conduct to a goal. Numerous definitions of what is indefinable

have been endeavored by psychologists, of which the slightest unsatisfactory are;

- The ability to meet novel circumstances, or to figure out how to do as such, by new versatile reactions
- "The capacity to perform tests or assignments, including the getting a handle on of relationships, the level of intelligence being corresponding to the multifaceted nature, or the dynamics, or both, of the relationship." J. Drover

11. "Intelligence

- A: the organic substrate of mental capacity, the brains' neuroanatomy and physiology; Intelligence
- B: the appearance of intelligence
- A, everything that impacts its look, all things considered, conduct; Intelligence
- C: the level of execution on psychometric trial of intellectual capacity." H. J. Eysenck

12. "Tactile abilities, capacity with respect to perceptual acknowledgment, quickness, range or adaptability or association, facility and creative energy, traverse of consideration, speed or sharpness accordingly." F. N. Freeman

13. "adaptation or adjustment of the person to his aggregate surroundings, or restricted viewpoints thereof, the ability to rearrange one's conduct designs to act all the more adequately and all the more properly in novel circumstances, the capacity to take in, the degree to which a man is educable, the capacity to bear on conceptual considering, the successful utilization of ideas and images in managing an issue to be illuminated" W. Freeman

14. "Intelligence is the capacity to tackle issues, or to make items, that are esteemed inside at least one cultural settings." H. Gardner

15. "Playing out an operation on a particular kind of substance to deliver a specific item." J. P. Guilford

16. "Sensation, discernment, affiliation, memory, creative ability, segregation, judgment and thinking." N. E. Haggerty

17. "The ability with respect to learning, and information possessed."A. C. Henson

18. "Subjective capacity." R. J. Herrnstein and C. Murray

19. "the resultant of the way toward gaining, putting away in memory, recovering, consolidating, looking at, and utilizing as a part of new settings data and applied abilities." Humphreys20. "Intelligence is the ability to learn, exercise judgment, and be imaginative."J. Huarte

21. "Intelligence is a general variable that goes through a wide range of performance."A. Jensen

22. "Intelligence is digestion to the degree that it joins all the given information of

experience inside its system, There can be most likely either, that mental life is likewise settlement to the environment. Absorption can never be immaculate in light of the fact that by fusing new components into its prior schemata the intelligence continually changes the last keeping in minds the end goal to conform them to new components." J. Piaget

23. "Capacity to adjust satisfactorily to generally new circumstances in life."R. Pinter

24. "A natural component by which the impacts of a many-sided quality of jolts are united and given a to some degree bound together impact in conduct." J. Peterson

25. "Certain arrangement of subjective abilities that empower a person to adjust and flourish in any given environment they end up in, and those psychological limits incorporate things like memory and recovery, and critical thinking et cetera. There's a bunch of intellectual capacities

that prompt to effective adjustment to an extensive variety of situations." D. K. Simonton

26. "Intelligence is a piece of the inner environment that shows through at the interface amongst individual and outside environment as a component of subjective assignment requests." R. E. Snow

27. "I want to allude to it as 'fruitful Intelligence.' And the reason is that the accentuation is on the utilization of your Intelligence to make progress in your life. So I characterize it as your expertise in accomplishing whatever it is you need to achieve in your life inside your socio-cultural setting implying that individuals have diverse objectives for themselves, and for some it's to get decent evaluations in school and to do well on tests, and for others it may be to wind up a decent ball player or on-screen character or performer." R. J. Sternberg

28. "The capacity to embrace exercises that are portrayed by (1) dif-Faculty (2) many-sided quality (3) dynamics (4) economy (5) adjusted ness to objective (6) social esteem (7) the rise of firsts, and to keep up such exercises under conditions that request a convergence of vitality and an imperviousness to enthusiastic strengths." Stoddard

29. "The capacity to bear on conceptual considering." L. M. Terman

30. "Intelligence, considered as a mental attribute, is the ability to make driving forces central at their initial, unfinished phase of arrangement. Intelligence is in this way the ability with respect to reflection, which is an inhibitory procedure." L. L. Thurston

31. "The ability to hinder an instinctual change, the ability to reclassify the repressed natural alteration in the light of comprehensibly experienced experimentation and the ability to

understand the adjusted intuitive modification in clear conduct to the benefit of the person as a social creature." L. L. Thurston

32. "A worldwide idea that includes an individual's capacity to act deliberately, thinks sanely, and bargains adequately with nature." D. Wechsler

33. "The ability to procure ability." H. Woodrow

34. "The term intelligence assigns an intricately interrelated gathering of capacities, nobody of which is totally or precisely known in man" R. M. Yerkes & A. W. Yerkes

35. "That workforce of psyche by which request is seen in a circumstance already viewed as disarranged." R. W. Youthful

Theories of Intelligence

Theories of intelligence, similar to the case with most logical speculations, have developed through a progression of models.

Four of the most persuasive standards have been mental estimation, otherwise called psychological measurement; subjective brain science, which worries about the procedures by which the mind capacities; cognitivism and conceptualism, a joined approach that studies the cooperation between the environment and mental procedures; and natural science, which considers the neural bases of intelligence. What takes after is a talk of advancements inside these four territories.

Psychometric Theories

Psychometric theories have for the most part looked to comprehend the structure of intelligence: What frame does it take, and what are its parts, assuming any? Such speculations have for the most part been founded on and set up by information acquired from trial of mental capacities, including analogies (e.g., legal counselor is to client as doctor is to), characterizations (e.g., Which word does not have a place with the others? robin, sparrow, chicken, blue jay), and arrangement fulfillments (e.g., What number comes next in the accompanying arrangement? 3, 6, 10, 15, 21).

Psychometric hypotheses depend on a model that depicts intelligence as a composite of capacities measured by mental tests. This model can be evaluated. For instance, execution on a number-arrangement test may speak to a weighted composite of number, reasoning, and memory capacities for a mind boggling arrangement. Scientific models take into account shortcoming in one territory to be counterbalanced by solid capacity in another range of test execution. Along these lines, predominant capacity in reasoning can make up for an inadequacy in number capacity.

The American psychologist L.L. Thurston couldn't help contradicting Spearman's theory, contending rather that there were seven variables, which he recognized as the "essential mental capacities." These seven capacities, as per Thurston, were verbal cognizance (as included in the learning of vocabulary and in perusing), verbal familiarity (as included in composing and in creating words), number (as included in fathoming genuinely straightforward numerical calculation and arithmetical thinking issues), spatial representation (as included in envisioning and controlling items, for example, fitting an arrangement of bags into a vehicle trunk), inductive thinking (as included in finishing a number arrangement or in anticipating the future on the premise of past experience), memory (as included in reviewing individuals' names or confronts, and perceptual speed (as included in quick editing to find typographical blunders in a content).

In spite of the fact that the verbal confrontation amongst Spearman and Thurston has stayed uncertain, different psychologists, for example, Canadian Philip E. Vernon and American Raymond B. Catelli—have proposed that both were appropriate in a few regards. Vernon and

Catelli saw scholarly capacities as progressive, with g, or general capacity, situated at the highest point of the chain of command. In any case, underneath g are levels of bit by bit narrowing capacities, finishing with the particular capacities distinguished by Spearman. Catelli, for instance, proposed in Abilities: Their Structure, Growth, and Action (1971) that general capacity can be subdivided into two further sorts, "liquid" and "solidified." Fluid capacities are the thinking and critical thinking capacities measured by tests, for example, analogies, characterizations, and arrangement culminations. Solidified capacities, which are thought to get from liquid capacities, incorporate vocabulary, general data, and learning about particular fields. The American psychologist John L. Horn proposed that solidified capacities pretty much increment over a man's life expectancy, though liquid capacities increment in prior years and abatement in later ones.

Most psychologists concurred that Spearman's subdivision of capacities was excessively limited; however not all concurred that the subdivision ought to be progressive. The American psychologist Joy Paul Guilford proposed a structure-of-intellect theory, which in its prior forms hypothesized 120 capacities. In The Nature of Human Intelligence (1967), Guilford contended that capacities can be partitioned into five sorts of operation, four sorts of substance, and six sorts of item. These features can be differently joined to shape 120 separate capacities. A case of such a capacity would be discernment (content) of semantic (content) relations (item), which would be included in perceiving the connection amongst lawyer and client in the similarity issue above (lawyer is to client as doctor is to). Guilford later expanded the quantity of capacities proposed by his theory to 150.

In the end it got to be obvious that there were major issues with the fundamental way to deal with psychometric theory. A development that had begun by hypothesizing one critically had come, in one of its significant appearances, to perceive 150. Additionally, the psychometricians (as practitioners of element examination were called) did not have a logical method for determining their disparities. Any technique that could bolster such a variety of theories appeared to be to some degree suspect. Most vital, be that as it may, the psychometric theories neglected to say anything substantive in regards to the procedures fundamental intelligence. It is one thing to talk about "general ability" or "liquid ability" yet very another to depict exactly what is going on in individuals' brains when they are practicing the capacity being referred to. The answer for these issues, as proposed by psychological analysts, was to concentrate straightforwardly the mental procedures fundamental intelligence and, maybe, to relate them to the features of intelligence placed by psychometricians.

The American psychologist John B. Carroll, in Human Cognitive Abilities (1993), proposed a "three-stratum" psychometric model of intelligence that developed existing speculations of intelligence. Numerous analysts view Carroll's model as complete, in light of the fact that it is endless supply of several information sets. In the principal stratum, Carroll recognized thin capacities (around 50 in number) that incorporated the seven essential abilities distinguished by Thurston. As indicated by Carroll, the center stratum included expansive capacities (around 10, for example, learning, recovery capacity, quickness, visual recognition, liquid intelligence, and the generation of thoughts. The third stratum comprised exclusively of the general component, g, as distinguished by Spearman. It may appear to be plainly obvious that the component at the top would be the general factor; however it is not, since there is no assurance that there is any general factor by any means.

Both customary and present day psychometric theories confront certain issues. Initially, it has not been demonstrated that a genuinely broad capacity incorporating all mental abilities really exists. In The General Factor of Intelligence: How General Is It? (2002), altered by the psychologists Robert Sternberg and Elena Grigorenko, benefactors to the altered volume gave contending perspectives of the g factor, with numerous proposing that particular abilities are more imperative than a general capacity, particularly on the grounds that they all the more promptly clarify singular varieties in scholarly working. Second, psychometric speculations can't correctly portray all that goes ahead in the brain. Third, it is not clear whether the tests on which psychometric theories are based are similarly fitting in all societies. Truth be told, there is a suspicion that effective execution on a trial of intelligence or cognitive ability will rely on upon one's nature with the cultural structure of the individuals who composed the test. In her

1997 paper "You Can't Take It with You: Why Ability Assessments Don't Cross Cultures," the American psychologist Patricia M. Greenfield inferred that a solitary test may quantify distinctive capacities in various societies. Her discoveries accentuated the significance of considering issues of cultural generality while making abilities tests.

Cognitive Theories

Amid the period commanded by psychometric theories, the investigation of intelligence was impacted most by those examining singular contrasts in individuals' test scores. In a deliver to the American Psychological Association in 1957, the American researcher Lee Cronbach, a pioneer in the testing field, censured the absence of shared view between analysts who concentrated on individual contrasts and the individuals who considered shared characteristics in human conduct. Cronbach's supplication to join the "two controls of logical brain research" drove, to some degree, to the advancement of cognitive theories of intelligence and of the fundamental procedures set by these theories.

Reasonable appraisals of execution require a comprehension of the procedures fundamental intelligence; generally, there is a danger of landing at conclusions that are deceiving, if not just wrong, while assessing general test scores or different evaluations of execution. Assume, for instance, that an understudy performs ineffectively on the verbal analogies addresses in a psychometric test. One conceivable conclusion is that the understudy does not reason well. A similarly conceivable translation, in any case, is that the understudy does not comprehend the words or can't read them in any case. An understudy who neglects to illuminate the relationship "venturesome is to pusillanimous as alleviate is to" may be a fantastic reasoner yet have just a humble vocabulary, or the other way around. By utilizing cognitive examination, the test translator can decide how much the poor score originates from low reasoning ability and how much it comes about because of not comprehension the words.

Fundamental most cognitive approaches to deal with intelligence is the supposition that intelligence involves mental representations, (for example, suggestions or pictures) of data and procedures that can work on such representations. A more intelligent individual is expected to speak to data all the more plainly and to work quicker on these representations. Researchers have looked to gauge the speed of different sorts of considering. Through scientific displaying, they partition the general time required to play out an assignment into the constituent times expected to execute each mental procedure. More often than not, they accept that these procedures are executed serially (in a steady progression) and, consequently, that the preparing times are added substance. Be that as it may, a few Researchers take into account parallel preparing, in which more than one process is executed in the meantime. Despite the kind of model utilized, the basic unit of analysis is a similar that of a mental procedure following up on a mental representation.

Various cognitive theories of intelligence have been created. Among them is that of the American analysts Earl B. Chase, Nancy Frost, and Clifford E. Luneburg, who in 1973 indicated one route in which psychometrics and cognitive modeling could be joined. Rather than beginning with ordinary psychometric tests, they started with errands that experimental psychologists were utilizing as a part of their laboratories to concentrate on the basic phenomena of cognition, for example, discernment, learning, and memory. They demonstrated that individual contrasts in these undertakings, which had at no other time been considered important, were in reality related (albeit fairly weakly) to examples of individual contrasts in psychometric intelligence test scores. Their outcomes proposed that the fundamental cognitive procedures are the building pieces of intelligence.

The accompanying case outlines the sort of assignment Hunt and his partners contemplated in their analysis: the subject is demonstrated a couple of letters, for example, "An," "an "or" A b." The subject's undertaking is to react as fast as would be prudent to one of two inquiries: "Are the two letters the same physically?" or "Are the two letters the same just in name?" In the primary combine the letters are the same physically, and in the second match the letters are the same just in name.

The psychologists hypothesized that a basic ability fundamental intelligence is the quick recovery of lexical data, for example, letter names, from memory. Thus, they were occupied with the time expected to respond to the question about letter names. By subtracting the response time to the question about physical match from the response time to the question about name coordinate, they could separate and put aside the time required for sheer speed of perusing letters and pushing catches on a PC. They found that the score contrasts appeared to anticipate psychometric test scores, particularly that on trial of verbal capacity, for example, perusing cognizance. Chase, Frost, and Luneburg reasoned that verbally easy individuals are the individuals who can ingest and after that recover from memory a lot of verbal data in short measures of time. The time factor was the noteworthy development in this research.

A couple of years after the fact, Sternberg proposed an option approach that could resolve the powerless connection between cognitive tasks and psychometric test scores. He contended that Hunt and his associates had tried for errands that were restricted to low-level cognitive processes. Albeit such procedures might be involved in intelligence, Sternberg claimed that they were fringe instead of focal. He prescribed that psychologists consider the assignments found on intelligence tests and afterward recognize the mental procedures and techniques individuals use to play out those tasks.

Sternberg started his study with the analogies referred to prior: "lawyer is to client as doctor is to." He established that the answer for such analogies requires an arrangement of segment cognitive processes that he distinguished as takes after: encoding of the similarity terms (e.g., recovering from memory characteristics of the terms lawyer provides professional services to a client, etc); gathering the connection between the initial two terms of the similarity (e.g., making sense of that a lawyer provides professional services to a client); mapping this connection to the second 50% of the similarity (e.g., making sense of that both a lawyer and a doctor provide professional services); applying this connection to produce a finishing (e.g., understanding that the individual to whom a doctor provides professional services is a patient); and afterward reacting. By applying mathematical modeling techniques to response time information, Sternberg secluded the parts of data preparing. He figured out if each trial subject did, in fact, utilize these procedures, how the procedures were consolidated, to what extent every procedure took, and how powerless every procedure was to blunder. Sternberg later demonstrated that the same cognitive processes are included in a wide assortment of scholarly assignments. He in this way presumed these and other related procedures underlie scores on intelligence tests.

An alternate approach was taken in the work of the British psychologist Ian Diary, among others. He contended that review time is an especially valuable method for measuring intelligence. It is imagined that individual contrasts in intelligence may get to some extent from contrasts in the rate of admission and preparing of basic boost data. In the examination time errand, a man takes a gander at two vertical lines of unequal length and is solicited to recognize which from the two is longer. Examination time is the time span of jolt presentation every individual needs with a specific end goal to separate which of the two lines is the longest. Some exploration proposes that more intelligent people can segregate the lengths of the lines in shorter examination times.

Other cognitive psychologists have examined human intelligence by developing computer models of human comprehension. Two pioneers in this field were the American computer experts Allen Newell and Herbert A. Simon. In the late 1950 and mid 1960, they worked with computer expert Cliff Shaw to develop a computer model of human problem solving. Called the General Problem Solver, it could discover answers for an extensive variety of genuinely organized issues, for example, logical proofs and numerical word issues. This exploration, in view of a heuristic method called ""means-ends analysis," drove Newell and Simon to propose a general theory of problem solving in 1972.

The vast majority of the issues contemplated by Newell and Simon were genuinely very much organized, in that it was conceivable to recognize a discrete arrangement of steps that would lead from the earliest starting point to the end of an issue. Different agents have been worried with different sorts of issues, for example, how a content is fathomed or how individuals are helped to remember things they definitely know when reading a text. The psychologists Marcel Just and Patricia Carpenter, for instance, demonstrated that muddled intelligence-test items, for example, figural matrix issues including prevailing upon geometric shapes, could be comprehended by a refined computer program at a level of exactness similar to that of human test takers. It is along these lines that a computer reflects a sort of "intelligence" like that of people. One critical difference, however, is that developers structure the issues for the computer, and they additionally compose the code that empowers the computer to take care of the issues. People "encode" their own particular data and don't have individual software engineers dealing with the procedure for them. To the degree that there is a "software engineer," it is in certainty the individual's own mind.

The majority of the cognitive theories depicted so far depend on what analysts call the "serial processing of data," implying that in these illustrations, cognitive processes are executed in arrangement, in a steady progression. However the suspicion that individual's procedure lumps of data each one in turn might be mistaken. Numerous psychologists have proposed rather that cognitive processing is fundamentally parallel. It has demonstrated troublesome, be that as it may, to recognize serial and parallel models of data processing (generally as it had been troublesome before to recognize distinctive factor models of human intelligence). Advanced techniques of numerical and computer demonstrating were later connected to this issue. Conceivable arrangements have included "parallel conveyed processing" models of the brain, as proposed by the analysts David E. Rumelhart and Jay L. McClelland. These models proposed that numerous sorts of data handling happen inside the brain on the double, as opposed to only each one in turn.

Computer modeling has yet to determine some real issues in comprehension the way of intelligence, in any case. For instance, the American psychologist Michael E. Cole and different psychologists have contended that cognitive processing does not suit the likelihood that portrayals of intelligence may vary starting with one culture then onto the next and crosswise over cultural subgroups. In addition, basic experience has demonstrated that traditional tests, despite the fact that they may foresee scholarly execution, can't dependably anticipate the path in which intelligence will be connected (i.e., through execution in occupations or other life circumstances past school). In acknowledgment of the contrast between genuine and scholarly execution, then, psychologists have come to study cognition not in isolation but rather with regards to the environment in which it works.

Cognitive-Contextual Theories

Cognitive-contextual theories manage the way that cognitive processes work in different settings. Two of the real theories of this sort are that of the American psychologist Howard Gardner and that of Sternberg. In 1983 Gardner challenged the assumption of a single intelligence by proposing a theory of "multiple intelligence." Earlier theorists had gone so far as to contend that intelligence comprises multiple abilities. Yet, Gardner went one stage more distant, contending that intelligence are multiple and include and incorporate, at a minimum, linguistic, logical-mathematical, spatial, musical, bodily-kinesthetic, interpersonal, and intrapersonal intelligence.

A portion of the intelligences proposed by Gardner looked like the capacities proposed by psychometric theorists, however others didn't. For instance, the possibility of a musical intelligence was moderately new, similar to the possibility of a bodily-kinesthetic intelligence, which enveloped the specific capacities of competitors and artists. Gardner determined his arrangement of intelligences essentially from investigations of cognitive processing, brain damage, exceptional individuals, and cognition across cultures. He likewise hypothesized on the likelihood of an existential intelligence (a concern with "ultimate" issues, for example, the importance of life), in spite of the fact that he was not able disengage a region of the mind that was committed to the thought of such inquiries. Gardner's research on multiple intelligences drove him to claim that most ideas of intelligence had been ethnocentric and culturally biased however that his was all inclusive, in light of the fact that it was based upon biological and multicultural information and also upon information got from the cognitive performance of a wide exhibit of individuals.

An option approach that assessed cognition and cultural setting was Sternberg's "triarchic" theory, which he proposed in Beyond IQ: A Triarchic Theory of Human Intelligence (1985). Both Gardner and Sternberg trusted that customary thoughts of intelligence were excessively limited; Sternberg, nonetheless, addressed how far psychologists ought to go past conventional ideas, recommending that musical and bodily-kinesthetic abilities are gifts as opposed to intelligences since they are genuinely particular and are not requirements for adjustment in many cultures.

Sternberg set three ("triarchic") coordinated and reliant parts of intelligence, which are concerned, separately, with a man's inner world, the outer world, and experience. The principal angle includes the cognitive processes and representations that frame the center of all idea. The second angle comprises of the utilization of these procedures and representations to the outside world. The triarchic theory holds that more-intelligent people are not only the individuals who can execute numerous cognitive processes rapidly or well; rather, their more prominent intelligence is reflected in knowing their qualities and shortcomings and promoting upon their qualities while adjusting for their shortcomings. More-intelligent people, then, discover a specialty in which they can work generally effectively. The third part of intelligence comprises of the coordination of the inside and outside universes through experience. This incorporates the capacity to apply already learned data to new or completely disconnected circumstances.

A few psychologists trust that intelligence is reflected in a capacity to adapt to generally novel circumstances. This clarifies why experience can be so critical. For instance, intelligence may be measured by setting individuals in a new culture and surveying their capacity to adapt to the new circumstance. As per Sternberg, another feature of experience that is essential in assessing knowledge is the automatization of cognitive processing, which happens when a moderately novel undertaking gets comfortable. The more a man automatizes the errands of everyday life, the more mental assets he will have for adapting to curiosity.

Different intelligences were proposed in the late twentieth century. In 1990 the psychologists John Mayer and Peter Salovey defined the term emotional intelligence as the capacity to see feelings, to get to and create feelings in order to help thought, to understand emotions and emotional knowledge, and to reflectively regulate emotions, and to brilliantly manage feelings in order to advance emotional and intellectual development.

The four angles recognized by Mayer and Salovey include

(a) Recognizing one's own particular emotions and in addition the emotions of others

(b) Applying emotions properly to encourage reasoning

(c) Understanding complex emotions and their impact on succeeding emotional states

(d) Having the capacity to deal with one's emotions and in addition those of others. The idea of emotional intelligence was advanced by the psychologist and columnist Daniel Goleman in books published from the 1990. A few tests created to measure emotional intelligence have demonstrated unobtrusive connections between emotional intelligence and conventional intelligence.

Biological Theories

The theories talked about above look to comprehend intelligence regarding hypothetical mental constructs, whether they are factors, cognitive processes, or cognitive processes in collaboration with setting.

Biological theories speak to a profoundly extraordinary approach that forgoes mental develops through and through. Promoters of such theories, for the most part called reductionists, trust that a genuine comprehension of intelligence is conceivable just by distinguishing its biological premise. Some would contend that there is no contrasting option to reductionism if, truth be told, the objective is to disclose as opposed to only to depict conduct. Be that as it may, the case is not an open-and-close one, particularly if intelligence is seen as something more than the insignificant processing of data. As Howard Gardner distinctly asked in the article "What We Do & Don't Know about Learning" (2004):

Can human learning and supposing be sufficiently diminished to the operations of neurons, from one perspective, or to chips of silicon, on the other? On the other hand is something critical missing, something that requires a clarification at the level of the human living being? Analogies that contrast the human brain to a computer recommend that biological ways to deal with intelligence ought to be seen as corresponding to, instead of as supplanting, different methodologies. For instance, when a man takes in another German vocabulary word, he gets to be mindful of a matching, say, between the German expression Die Farbe and the English word color, yet a follow is likewise set down in the cerebrum that can be gotten to when the data is required. Albeit generally little is thought about the biological bases of intelligence, advance has been made on three unique fronts, all including investigations of cerebrum operation.

Hemispheric Studies

One biological approach has heaps of intellectual performance as they identify with the regions of the mind from which they start. In her exploration on the functions of the cerebrum's two sides of the equator, the psychologist Jerri Levy and others found that the left hemisphere is predominant in analytical tasks, for example, are included in the utilization of dialect, while the right side of the equator is prevalent in numerous types of visual and spatial errands. By and large, the right half of the globe has a tendency to be more manufactured and comprehensive in its working than the left. By the by, examples of hemispheric specialization are perplexing and can't undoubtedly be summed up.

The specialization of the two halves of the globe of the mind is exemplified in an early study by Levy and the American neurobiologist Roger W. Sperry, who worked with split-mind calm that is, individuals whose corpus callosum had been separated. Since the corpus callosum joins the two sides of the equator in a conventional mind, in these patients the halves of the globe work openly of each other. Impose and Sperry asked for that split-mind patients hold minimal wooden pieces, which they couldn't see, in either their left or their right hand and to match them with looking at two-dimensional pictures. They found that patients using the left hand enhanced at this endeavor than those using the benefit; in the meantime, of more interest, they found that the two social affairs of patients appeared to use unmistakable methodologies in handling the issue. Their analysis displayed that the right hand (told by the left 50% of the globe of the mind) worked better with illustrations that are immediately depicted in words however are difficult to isolate ostensibly. On the other hand, the left hand (managed by the right half of the equator) was more talented with cases requiring visual partition.

Brain Wave Studies

A moment front of biological research has included the utilization of brain-wave recordings. The German-conceived British psychologist Hans Eysenck, for instance, contemplated brain examples and speed of reaction in individuals taking intelligence tests. Prior brain-wave inquire about had considered the connection between these waves and execution on capacity tests or in different cognitive undertakings. Scientists in some of these studies found a relationship between specific parts of electroencephalogram (EEG) waves, occasion related-potential (ERP) waves, and scores on a standard psychometric trial of intelligence.

Blood Flow Studies

A third and later front of research includes the measurement of blood stream in the brain, which is a genuinely coordinate marker of useful movement in brain tissue. In such studies the sum and area of blood stream in the brain is observed while subjects perform cognitive errands. The psychologist John Horn, an unmistakable scientist around there, found that more established grown-ups demonstrate diminished blood stream to the brain, that such reductions are more prominent in a few regions of the brain than in others, and that the abatements are especially remarkable in those zones in charge of close fixation, unconstrained readiness, and the encoding of new data. Utilizing positron discharge tomography (PET), the psychologist Richard Haier found that individuals who perform better on routine intelligence tests regularly demonstrate less enactment in pertinent bits of the brain than do the individuals who perform less well. Furthermore, neurologists Antonio Damasio and Hannah Damasio and their partners utilized PET outputs and attractive reverberation imaging (MRI) to study brain work in subjects performing critical thinking assignments. These discoveries asserted the significance of comprehension intelligence as a workforce that creates after some time.

Development of Intelligence

There have been various ways to deal with the investigation of the advancement of intelligence. Psychometric theorists, for example, have tried to see how intelligence creates as far as changes in intelligence factors and in different capacities in adolescence. For instance, the idea of mental age was well known amid the principal half of the twentieth century. A given mental age was held to speak to a normal kid's level of mental working for a given sequential age. In this manner, a normal 12-year-old would have a mental age of 12, however an above-normal 10-year-old or a beneath normal 14-year-old may likewise have a mental age of 12 years. The idea of mental age fell into disapproval, notwithstanding, for two clear reasons. Initially, the idea does not appear to work after about the age of 16. The mental test execution of, say, a 25-year-old is by and large no superior to that of a 24-or 23-year-old, and in later adulthood some test scores appear to begin declining. Second, numerous psychologists trust that scholarly advancement does not display the sort of smooth congruity that the idea of mental age seems to suggest. Or maybe, improvement appears to come in discontinuous blasts, whose planning can contrast starting with one youngster then onto the next.

The Work of Jean Piaget

The point of interest work in scholarly improvement in the twentieth century got not from psychometrics but rather from the convention built up by the Swiss psychologist Jean Piaget. His hypothesis was worried with the systems by which scholarly improvement happens and the periods through which kids create. Piaget trusted that the kid investigates the world and watches regularities and makes speculation much as a researcher does. Scholarly improvement, he contended, gets from two cognitive procedures that work in to some degree corresponding style. The main, which he called absorption, fuses new data into an officially existing cognitive structure. The second, whom he called settlement, frames another cognitive structure into which new data can be consolidated. The process of assimilation is illustrated in simple problem-solving tasks. Suppose that a child knows how to solve problems that require calculating a percentage of a given number. The child then learns how to solve problems that ask what percentage of a number another number is. The child already has a cognitive structure, or what Piaget called a "schema," for percentage problems and can incorporate the new knowledge into the existing structure.

Assume that the tyke is then requested that figure out how to tackle time-rate-separate issues, having at no other time managed this sort of issue. This would include convenience the development of another cognitive structure. Cognitive improvement, as indicated by Piaget, speaks to a dynamic harmony between the two procedures of absorption and settlement.

As a moment piece of his theory, Piaget hypothesized four noteworthy periods in individual scholarly advancement. The main, the sensor engine period, reaches out from birth through general age two. Amid this period, a tyke figures out how to alter reflexes to make them more versatile, to arrange activities, to recover concealed items, and, in the long run, to start speaking to data rationally. The second time frame, known as preoperational, runs roughly from age two to age seven. In this period a tyke creates dialect and mental symbolism and figures out how to concentrate on single perceptual measurements, for example, color and size. The third, the solid operational period, ranges from about age 7 to age 12. Amid this time a youngster grows purported protection abilities, which empower him to perceive that things that may give off an impression of being distinctive are really similar that will be, that their key properties are "rationed." For instance, assume that water is poured from a wide short measuring glass into a tall slender one. A preoperational kid, asked which measuring glass has more water, will state that the second receptacle does (the tall thin one); a solid operational youngster, in any case, will perceive that the measure of water in the containers must be the same. At long last, youngsters rise into the fourth, formal operational period, which starts at about age 12 and proceeds all through life. The formal-operational kid creates thinking aptitudes in every single consistent blend and figures out how to think with unique ideas. For instance, a kid in the solid operational period will have incredible trouble deciding all the conceivable orderings of four digits, for example, 3-7-5-8. The tyke who has achieved the formal operational stage, in any case, will embrace a strategy of systematically fluctuating shifts of digits, beginning maybe with the last digit and progressing in the direction of the first. This efficient state of mind is not regularly feasible for those in the solid operational period.

Piaget's theory majorly affected the perspectives of intellectual improvement, yet it is not as generally acknowledged today as it was in the mid-twentieth century. One deficiency is that the theory bargains principally with scientific and logical methods of thought, along these lines dismissing stylish, instinctive, and different modes. Moreover, Piaget failed in that youngsters were generally fit for performing mental operations sooner than the ages at which he assessed they could perform them.

Post Piaget Theories

In spite of its reduced impact, Piaget's theory keeps on serving as a reason for different perspectives. One theory has developed Piaget's work by proposing a conceivable fifth, grown-up, time of advancement, for example, "issue discovering." Problem discovering precedes critical thinking; it is the way toward distinguishing issues that merit understanding in any case. A moment course has distinguished times of improvement that are entirely unique in relation to those proposed by Piaget. A third course has been to acknowledge the times of advancement Piaget proposed yet to hold that they have diverse cognitive bases. A portion of the hypotheses in the third gathering stress the significance of memory limit. For instance, it has been demonstrated those kids' challenges in taking care of transitive deduction issues, for example,

On the off chance that A is more prominent than B, B is more prominent than C, and D is not as much as C, which is the greatest? Result essentially from memory restrictions as opposed to thinking impediments (as Piaget had contended). A fourth course has been to concentrate on the part of knowledge being developed. A few specialists contend that quite a bit of what has been credited to thinking and critical thinking capacity in intellectual improvement is entirely ascribed to the degree of the kid's knowledge.

The Environmental Viewpoint

The perspectives of intellectual improvement portrayed most importantly accentuate the significance of the person in intellectual advancement. Be that as it may, an options perspective underlines the significance of the individual's environment, especially his social environment. This view is identified with the cognitive-relevant hypotheses talked about above. Championed initially by the Russian psychologist L.S. Vygotsky, this perspective recommends that intellectual advancement might be to a great extent affected by a youngster's communications with others: a tyke sees others supposing and acting in certain ways and after that disguises and models what is seen. An elaboration of this view is the proposal by the Israeli psychologist Reuven Feuerstein that the way to intellectual improvement is the thing that he called "interceded learning background." The parent intervenes, or translates, the environment for the tyke, and it is generally through this intercession that the tyke figures out how to comprehend and decipher the world.

The part of the environment is especially obvious in studies crosswise over societies. In her examination on the social settings of intelligence, Greenfield, while considering indigenous Mayan individuals, found that the Mayan origination of intelligence is significantly more group than the origination of intelligence in European or North American societies. To the Maya, a lot of being clever includes having the capacity to work with others successfully. Furthermore, the psychologist Elena Grigorenko and her partners, in "The Organization of Lou Conceptions of Intelligence: A Study of Implicit Theories in a Kenyan Village" (2001), found that country Kenyans have a wide origination of intelligence that underscores moral conduct, especially obligation to others.

Youngsters who experience childhood in environments that don't stretch Western standards of education will be unable to show their capacities on ordinary Western intelligence tests. Sternberg and others have found that rustic Tanzanian youngsters performed much better on skills tests when they were given amplified direction past the typical test guidelines. Without this extra guideline, notwithstanding the youngsters did not generally comprehend what they should do, and, due to this, they failed to meet expectations on the tests. Thus, a study in Kenya measured youngsters' knowledge of regular cures used to battle parasites and other basic sicknesses. Tests for this kind of knowledge were joined with the traditional Western trial of intelligence and scholarly accomplishment. Comes about demonstrated a negative connection between's useful intelligence (knowledge of therapeutic cures) and scholastic accomplishment. These discoveries proposed that in a few societies, scholarly skills may not be especially esteemed; thus, the brighter kids put more exertion in gaining down to earth skills.

Measuring Intelligence

All of the hypotheses talked about above utilize complex errands for gauging intelligence in both youngsters and grown-ups. After some time, theorists picked specific undertakings for breaking down human intelligence, some of which have been unequivocally examined here e.g., acknowledgment of analogies, a grouping of comparative terms, extrapolation of number arrangement, execution of transitive inductions, and so forth. Despite the fact that the sorts of complex errands talked about so far have a place with a solitary convention for the measurement of intelligence, the field really has two noteworthy customs. The convention that has been talked about most unmistakably and has been most compelling is that of the French psychologist Alfred Benet (1857–1911).

A prior convention and one that still demonstrates some impact upon the field is that of the English researcher Sir Francis Galton. Expanding on thoughts set forth by his uncle Charles Darwin in On the Origin of Species (1859), Galton trusted that human capacities could be comprehended through scientific examination. From 1884 to 1890 Galton kept up a research facility in London where guests could have themselves measured on an assortment of psychophysical undertakings, for example, weight segregation and affect the ability to musical pitch. Galton trusted that psychophysical capacities were the premise of intelligence and, henceforth, that these tests were measures of intelligence. The most punctual formal intelligence tests, in this manner, required a man to perform such basic assignments as choosing which of two weights was heavier or indicating how strongly one could press one's hand.

The Galtonian convention was taken to the United States by the American psychologist James McKean Catelli. Later, one of Chattel's understudies, the American anthropologist Clark Wissler, gathered information demonstrating that scores on Galtonian sorts of assignments were bad indicators of evaluations in school or even of scores on different errands. Castelli regardless kept on building up his Galtonian approach in psychometric research and, with

Edward Thorndike, set up middle for mental testing and measurement.

The IQ Test

The more powerful convention of mental testing was created by Benet and his colleague, Theodore Simon, in France. In 1904 the priest of the open guideline in Paris named a commission to think about or make tests that would guarantee that rationally impeded youngsters got a sufficient education. The pastor was likewise worried that offspring of ordinary intelligence were being set in classes for rationally hindered youngsters on account of conduct issues. Indeed, even before Wissler's exploration, Benet, who was accused of building up the new test, had straight rejected the Galtonian custom, trusting that Galton's tests measured minor capacities. He proposed rather that trial of intelligence ought to quantify skills, for example, judgment, cognizance, and thinking, similar sorts of skills measured by most intelligence tests today. Benet's initial test was taken to Stanford University by

Lewis Terman, whose adaptation came to be known as the Stanford-Benet test. This test has been reexamined every now and again and keeps on being utilized as a part of nations everywhere throughout the world.

The Stanford-Benet test, and others like it, has yielded no less than a general score alluded to as an intelligence remainder, or IQ. A few tests, for example, the Wechsler Adult Intelligence Scale (Revised) and the Wechsler Intelligence Scale for Children (Revised), yield a general IQ and also isolate IQs for verbal and execution subtests. A case of a verbal subtest would be vocabulary, while a case of an execution subtest would be picture course of action, the last requiring an examinee to organize an arrangement of pictures into a succession with the goal that they recount a fathomable story.

Later improvements in intelligence testing extended the scope of capacities tried. For instance, in 1997 the psychologists J.P. Das and Jack A. Naglieri distributed the

Cognitive Assessment System, a test in light of a theory of intelligence initially proposed by the Russian psychologist Alexander Luria. The test measured arranging capacities, purposeful capacities, and synchronous and progressive preparing capacities. Concurrent preparing capacities are utilized to settle assignments, for example, figural framework issues, in which the test taker must fill in a grid with a missing geometric shape. Progressive handling capacities are utilized as a part of tests, for example, digit traverse, in which one must rehash back a string of remembered digits.

IQ was initially processed as the proportion of mental age to chronological (physical) age, duplicated by 100. Accordingly, if an offspring of age 10 had a mental age of 12 (that is, performed on the test at the level of a normal 12-year-old), the kid was doled out an IQ of 12/10 × 100, or 120. On the off chance that the 10-year-old had a mental age of 8, the youngster's IQ would be 8/10 ×

100, or 80. A score of 100, where the mental age squares with the chronological age, is normal.

As talked about over, the idea of mental age has fallen into unsavoriness. Numerous tests still yield an IQ, however, they are regularly figured on the premise of actual circulations. The scores are allocated on the premise of what rate of individuals of a given gathering would be relied upon to have a specific IQ.

The Distribution of IQ Scores

Intelligence tests scores take after an around typical conveyance, implying that the vast majority score close to the center of the dissemination of scores and that scores drop off reasonably quickly in recurrence as one moves in either bearing from the middle. For instance, on the IQ scale, around 2 out of 3 scores fall somewhere around 85 and 115, and around 19 out of 20 scores fall somewhere around 70 and 130. Put another way, just 1 out of 20 scores contrasts from the normal IQ (100) by more than 30 focuses.

It has been normal to connect marks to specific levels of IQ. At the upper end, the mark talented is some of the time allotted to individuals with IQs of 130 or higher. Scores at the lower end have been given the names marginal impeded (70 to 84) and seriously hindered (25 to 39). Every single such term, in any case, has pitfalls and can be counterproductive. Initially, their utilization accepts that ordinary intelligence tests give adequate data to order somebody as talented or rationally impeded, however, most powers would dismiss this suspicion. Actually, the data yielded by customary intelligence tests speaks to just a genuinely limit scope of capacities. To name somebody as rationally hindered exclusively on the premise of a solitary test score, in this way, is to hazard doing an injury and a bad form to that individual. Most psychologists and different powers perceive that social and additionally entirely intellectual skills must be considered in any characterization of a mental impediment.

Second, skill is for the most part perceived as more than only a level of intelligence, even extensively characterized. Most psychologists who have concentrated on skilled people concur that an assortment of viewpoints makes up talent. Howard E. Gruber, a Swiss psychologist, and Mihaly Csikszentmihalyi, an American psychologist, were among the individuals who questioned that skill in youth is the sole indicator of grown-up capacities. Gruber held that talent unfurls throughout a lifetime and includes accomplishment at any rate as much as intelligence. Talented individuals, he battled, have life arranges that they try to acknowledge, and these arrangements create through the span of numerous years. As was valid in the exchange of mental impediment, the idea of skill is trivialized in the event that it is seen just as far as a solitary test score.

Third, the criticalness of a given test score can be diverse for various individuals. A specific IQ score may demonstrate a larger amount of intelligence for a man who experienced childhood in neediness and went to a lacking school than it would for a man who experienced childhood in an upper-white-collar class environment and was educated in a profitable learning environment. An IQ score on a test given in English likewise may demonstrate a more elevated amount of intelligence for a man whose first dialect is not English than it would for a local English speaker. Another viewpoint that influences the criticalness of test scores is that a few people are "test on the edge" and may do inadequately on any state sanctioned test. In view of these and comparable downsides, it has come to be trusted that scores ought to be deciphered painstakingly, on an individual premise.

Heritability & Malleability of Intelligence

Intelligence has generally been conceptualized as a pretty much-settled attribute. While a minority of specialists accepts either that it is very heritable or that it is negligible heritable, most take a middle of the road position.

Among the most productive techniques that have been utilized to survey the heritability of intelligence is the investigation of indistinguishable twins who were isolated at an early age and raised separated? In the event that the twins were brought up in discrete environments, and in the event that it is expected that when twins are isolated they are haphazardly dispersed crosswise over environments (regularly a questionable supposition), then the twins would have in like manner the greater part of their qualities yet none of their environment, with the exception of chance environmental cover. Accordingly, the connection between's their exhibitions on intelligence tests could recognize any conceivable connection between test scores and heredity. Another technique thinks about the relationship between intelligence-test scores of indistinguishable twins and those of friendly twins. Since these outcomes are figured on the premise of intelligence-test scores, nonetheless, they speak to just those parts of intelligence that are measured by the tests.

Investigations of twins do in actuality give solid confirmation to the heritability of intelligence; the scores of indistinguishable twins raised separated are exceptionally connected. Also, embraced kids' scores are exceptionally connected with their introduction to the world guardians and not with their new parents. Likewise critical are discoveries that heritability can vary amongst ethnic and racial gatherings, and in addition crosswise over time inside a solitary gathering; that is, the degree to which qualities versus environment matter in IQ relies on upon numerous factors, including financial class. Additionally, the psychologist Robert Plomin and others have found that confirmation of the heritability of intelligence increments with age; this recommends, as a man becomes more established, hereditary factors turn into an essential determinant of intelligence, while environmental factors turn out to be less imperative.

Whatever the heritability variable of IQ might be, it is a different issue whether intelligence can be expanded. Confirm that it can be given by the American-conceived New Zealand political researcher James Flynn, who demonstrated that intelligence test scores the world over rose relentlessly in the late twentieth century. The explanations behind the expansion are not completely sawed, nonetheless, and the marvel in this way requires extra cautious examination. Among numerous conceivable reasons for the expansion, for instance, are environmental changes, for example, the expansion of vitamin C to pre-birth and postnatal eating regimen and, all the more, for the most part, the enhanced sustenance of moms and newborn children as contrasted and before in the century. In their book, The Bell Curve (1994), Richard Herrnstein and Charles Murray contended that IQ is imperative forever achievement and that contrasts between racial gatherings in life achievement can be credited to a limited extent to contrasts in IQ. They conjectured that these distinctions may be hereditary. As noted above, such claims stay theoretical.

Regardless of the general increment in scores, normal IQs keep on varying both crosswise over nations and crosswise over various financial gatherings. For instance, numerous scientists have found a positive connection between's financial status and IQ, despite the fact that they differ about the explanations behind the relationship. Most examiners likewise concur that distinctions in educational open doors assume an essential part, however, some trust that the primary premise of the distinction is innate. There is no wide assertion regarding why such contrasts exist. Most critical, it ought to be noticed that these distinctions depend on

IQ alone and not on intelligence as it is more comprehensively characterized. Indeed, even less is referred to about gathering contrasts in intelligence as it is extensively characterized than is thought about contrasts in IQ. By the by, hypotheses of acquired contracts in IQ between racial gatherings have been observed to be without premise. There is more changeability inside gatherings than between gatherings.

At last, regardless of how heritable intelligence might be, a few parts of it are still pliant. With mediation, even an exceedingly heritable quality can be adjusted. A program of preparing in intellectual skills can build a few parts of a man's intelligence; notwithstanding, no preparation program—no environmental state of any kind—can make a virtuoso of a man with low measured intelligence. Yet, a few additions are conceivable, and programs have been produced for expanding intellectual skills. Intelligence, in the perspective of numerous powers, is not an inescapable result the day a man is conceived. A fundamental pattern for psychologists in the intelligence field has been to consolidate testing and preparing capacities to individuals benefit as much as possible from their intelligence.

The Nine Types of Intelligence

1. Naturist Intelligence (Nature Smart)

To assigns the human capacity to separate among living things like plants, animals and also affectability to different elements of the natural world such as clouds & rocks configuration. This capacity was obviously of significant worth in our transformative past as hunters, gatherers, and farmers; it keeps on being focal in such parts as botanist or chef. It is additionally estimated that a lot of our shopper society abuses the naturalist intelligence, which can be assembled in the segregation among autos, shoes, sorts of cosmetics, and so forth.

Nature smart individuals are agreeable in and flourish in natural settings. They appreciate hobbies that include nature like gardening and bird viewing. They may love to work with animals and have their own particular or volunteer at a creature protect. They may have a liking for perceiving and recollecting the names of various types of dogs or cats or distinctive names of birds or flowers or leaves.

Programming ideas for nature smart children:

- o Do a program on gardening or make a gardening club
- o Do a program on nature themes like space, weather, oceans, animals
- o Bring in natural items to upgrade programs. For example, for Book Trek we frequently acquire instruments from various nations that are produced using gourds or wood.
- o For an exploratory writing program, take kids outside to go out for a stroll

and diary about what they see and listen

- o Do makes that utilization natural components or do creates about nature subjects
- o Tell or read stories about nature
- o Bring in exceptional visitors that have this ability, possibly a neighborhood nursery worker, somebody who works at the zoo, somebody from a creature protect
- o Do a program on pets and pet care
- o Incorporate exercises that have children utilize their five detects

2. Musical Intelligence (Musical Smart)

Musical intelligence is the capacity to recognize pitch, cadence, timbre, and tone. This intelligence engages us to see, make, replicate, and consider music, as showed by arrangers, conductors, artists, vocalist, and delicate gathering of people individuals. Strikingly, there is routinely a loaded with feeling relationship among music and the sentiments; and scientific and musical intelligence may share ordinary derivation shapes. Young grown-ups with this sort of intelligence are for the most part singing or drumming to themselves. They are normally entirely mindful of sounds others may miss.

Individuals who are music smart live and inhale music. This may happen in a wide range of ways. A few people enjoy a wide range of sorts of music, can understand musical documentation, can evaluate sorts of music and discuss music in an in-depth way. Some get a kick out of the chance to make new instruments or figure out how to play an assortment of instruments. Some make their own specific verses and sing exhibitions or sing in choirs. Like the majority of the intelligence, there are a wide range of approaches to be music smart and somebody who may not be a good singer may be an incredible composer. Somebody who adores music may get a kick out of the chance to dance to express the sentiments that music cause yet won't have the capacity to play an instrument.

Kids who are music smart may grow up to be musicians, music commentators, composers, singers, sound engineers, producers, instrument makers, conductors, band or choir teachers, storytellers, poets, song or jingle writers, radio d.j.

Programming for Music Smart Learners

Music is anything but difficult to join in library programs regardless of the possibility that the leader isn't musically inclined. You don't need to sing in order or play an instrument to fuse music into projects (in spite of the fact that it can offer assistance!). It can be as basic as having music out of sight of a program.

Here is a summary of potential programming ideas:

- o Teach kids songs (particularly songs that have movements

- Bring in musical instruments from around the globe for children to get some answers concerning and play with
- Invite performers to the library to talk about their most adored sort of music or musical instrument
- Play music beyond anyone's ability to see
- Help kids to learn truths by putting them to music (for example, a program where you have some music that helps the Childs, take in the names of dinosaurs or dinosaur assurances)
- Narrate some stories or show picture books that incorporate tunes or have a musical plot
- Do a book program that has been made into a movie, play the soundtrack amid the program
- Teach kids diverse dance moves in Book Trek
- Play a delight like musical seats or musical stop games

- o Play diversions that have beat rhymes connected with them
- o Do a program on forming music verses or have children make raps in a program

3. Logical Mathematical Intelligence (Number/Reasoning Smart)

Logical mathematical intelligence is the capacity to figure, measure, consider recommendations and speculations, and do finish mathematical operations. It engages us to see associations and affiliations and to use rapid, run of the mill thought; progressive intuition abilities; and inductive and deductive hypothesis outlines. Logical intelligence is for the most part all around made in mathematicians, scientists, and examiners. Energetic adults with heaps of logical intelligence are possessed with cases, groupings, and associations. They are pulled in to number juggling issues, framework beguilements and trials. People who are logic smart acknowledge math, science, and logical considering. They get a kick out of the opportunity to work with numbers and codes and questions. They acknowledge essential thinking and handling complex activities. Schools are in like manner extraordinary in showing information in ways that logic smart youngsters get it.

Kids who are logic smart may grow up to be accountants, scientists, cooks, engineers, computer programmers, lawyers, chemists, astronauts, bankers, technical writers, meteorologists, engineers.

Programming for Logic Smart Learners

Making logic smart exercises can now and again be scaring particularly if it's not an intelligence that somebody is solid in but rather don't stress. There are numerous fun recreations and straightforward exercises that should be possible to incorporate this intelligence in library programming.

Here is a list of potential program ideas

- Do a program about codes
- Do a book examination on a chapter book that has codes in it like Chasing Vermeer by Blue Balliet or Harriet Tubman, Secret Agent by Thomas Allen
- Do a program about science experiments or incorporate science experiments into a current program
- Include games like tangrams, Sudoku, chess, checkers
- Use various types of maps to help kids find out about nations
- Ask addresses after a story to help kids review and thoroughly consider the story and its implications
- Use riddles
- If you're doing a sports program, discuss a few sports statistics
- Do a creative written work workshop about puzzles. For one of our creative written work workshops, two instructors lead a joint mystery composing workshop where a gathering of fifteen children worked

with the leaders to make one mystery story.

- o Do a cooking program
- o Do an astronomy program
- o Do a program on making sites, redoing their MySpace accounts, and other computer subjects
- o Do a program on spies and mystery specialists
- o Do a program on weather
- o Do any sort of nonfiction program and discuss statistics and examples that identify with that subject
- o Do an unravel a-mystery program where there are pieces of information and fortune maps
- o Do a forager chase
- o Include somebody moment or five-minute secrets into your program

4. Interpersonal Intelligence (People Smart)

The interpersonal intelligence is the capacity to comprehend and interface successfully with others. It incorporates convincing verbal and nonverbal correspondence, the ability to note refinements among others, affectability to the inclinations and demeanors of others, and the ability to draw in numerous perspectives, teachers, social workers, actors, and politicians all show interpersonal intelligence. Energetic adults with this kind of intelligence are pioneers among their partners, are awesome at giving, and seem to understand others' feelings and expectations. People's smart people exist together with others since they are tuned into others and their considerations and feelings. They get a kick out of the chance to associate with individuals in social settings and in volunteer, club, or sports exercises. They aren't hesitant to impart their insights and work with individuals to get everybody in agreement, since they can work with individuals and comprehend their thought processes and yearnings and how to speak with them, body smart individuals frequently make incredible leaders. They additionally may end up helping other people with their issues.

They might be a counselor, a politician, a CEO, a social activist, a server/server, an public speaker, a social worker, a marketing specialist, a salesman, or an educator.

Program Ideas for Interpersonal smart children

- o Group games that require teamwork
- o Improve activities
- o Reader's theater or skits
- o Experiments or crafts that energize working together
- o Scavenger hunts
- o Use volunteers in programs (this provides an extraordinary leadership opportunity for the teens and the more youthful kids truly admire them)
- o Do some pretending
- o Incorporate opportunities for kids to converse with each other in a gathering about books or diverse topics
- o Book Buddies (This is a program where youthful kids rehearse their perusing by perusing to high schooled

or grown-up buddies. Teens who are people smart will truly like this program.)

- o Read books that have people smart characters for books discussions or different programs

5. Bodily Kinesthetic Intelligence (Body Smart)

Bodily kinesthetic intelligence is the ability to control objects and use an assortment of physical skills. This intelligence additionally includes a feeling of timing and the perfection of abilities through mind–body union. Competitors, dancers, surgeons, and craftspeople show particularly developed genuine kinesthetic intelligence. Body Smart individuals might be practice focus teachers, mentors, sports players, craftsmen, dancers, actors, woodworkers, surgeons, woodworkers, or crafters like quilters or stone carvers.

Programming Ideas for Body Smart Kids

- Charades
- Songs with movements
- Stories that have actions and motions
- Games having motions and movements
- Science experiments requiring motions and movements
- Incorporate appear into a program; maybe do a theater show
- Do a sport gaming program (get competitors to talk about their game, run a games focus like a hand to hand fighting or yoga session)
- Do a bookopoly program (that have physical challenges requiring movements)
- Teach kids how to play the musical instruments utilizing their body

6. Linguistic Intelligence (Word Smart)

Linguistic intelligence is the capacity to think in words and to use dialect to express and acknowledge complex meanings. Linguistic intelligence allows us to understand the order and significance of words and to apply meta-linguistic skills to ponder our use of dialect. Linguistic intelligence is the most generally shared human ability and is clear in poets, novelists, journalists, and compelling open speakers. Youthful adults with this sort of intelligence appreciate writing, reading, telling stories or doing crossword puzzles.

People who are word smart love dialect, they might be a strong speller. They may love to peruse. They may love to compose. They might be a decent storyteller. Someone who is word smart may not necessarily have the capacity to peruse truly fast or spell truly well however he/she can spin an okay story. There is a wide range of ways to be word smart and someone who is word smart won't necessarily be great in each aspect of this intelligence.

Kids who are word smart may grow up to be writers, journalists, comedians, politicians, speechwriters, teachers, librarians, proofreaders, publicist/advertising specialists, radio or television announcers, and storytellers.

Programming for Word Smart Learners

In schools and in libraries making programs for word smart learners is presumably the easiest to do because the intelligence is used the most to show kids information. The trap is to take an action that is intended for kids who are word smart and to add some things to it that will also achieve different learners.

Here is a list of potential program ideas

- o Tell a joke (humor reaches everybody not just the word smart kids and humor is important for boys)
- o Do a skit or manikin show or pursuer's theater (in the event that you have kids go along with you in the skit that allows them to be a part of the story, to personalize it , and to move around)

- Teach kids how to be storytellers
- Tell a story (reading a story is incredible yet telling a story to kids, especially telling a story that you truly adore and interface with, will keep them spellbound)
- Read a story
- Talk to kids about the importance of a book (discussions after folktales can be extremely interesting. A great deal of kids will ask what it means and if the story is valid.)
- Invite guests to peruse their favorite story
- Bring in people who can read a story in an alternate dialect and after that discussion to the kids about it
- Tell a Kamishibai story (This is a Japanese storytelling strategy that includes a wooden stage and paper story cards.)
- Incorporate verse or finger play/activity rhymes into the program

- Randomly stop your program and shout, "Verse Break!" and read a favorite lyric.
- Book talk
- Do a creative writing movement or workshop
- Do a workshop about diary (if the kids make their diary that is a body smart movement. On the off chance that they write in them, that is a self smart action.)
- Do a book discussion
- Incorporate word games into a program

7. Intrapersonal Intelligence (Self Smart)

Intrapersonal intelligence is the ability to understand oneself and one's thoughts and feelings, and to use such knowledge in arranging and directioning one's life. Intrapersonal intelligence involves energy about the self, as well as of the human condition. It is clear in psychologist, spiritual leaders, and philosophers. These youthful adults might be shy. They are extremely mindful of their own feelings and are self-propelled.

Self smart people are comfortable with them and are knowledgeable about their strengths and weaknesses because they do self-reflection. They may jump at the chance to be by themselves to thoroughly consider an issue. They may wander off in fantasy land about their future, keep goals both short-term and long haul to accomplish, and attempt to get things done to develop as a person. Self smart people may exercise, eat healthy, as well as reflect. They may also have strong opinions about things and may do their own thing with regards to dress and personal behavior.

Self smart kids may grow up to be actors, comedians, artists, therapists, writers, professors, religious leaders, politicians or some other sort of pioneer like a CEO or activist.

Programming for Self Smart Learners

Here is a list of potential program ideas;

- o Have time amid a creative writing workshop for kids to work exclusively and afterward share their work toward the end
- o During a program permit kids time to ask questions or associate the story or action to their everyday life
- o Open-finished crafts can be an extraordinary path for kids to be introspective and choose what they need to make
- o Do a program on diary or creative nonfiction
- o Have programs that permit kids to be expressive through craftsmanship, through move, or through storytelling.
- o Read stories that have self-smart characters
- o Do a program on wellbeing like a yoga program or a nourishment program
- o If you incorporate a great deal of games in your programs, consider

including some that kids can play by themselves each once in for a short time

o Talk about how kids may feel about a story or discuss the feelings distinctive characters may have in the wake of reading or telling a story or amid a book discussion

8. Spatial Intelligence (Picture Smart)

Spatial intelligence is the capacity to think in three dimensions. Core capacities incorporate mental symbolism, spatial reasoning, picture control, graphic and artistic skills, and a dynamic creative energy. Sailors, pilots, sculptors, painters, and architects all display spatial intelligence. Youthful adults with this sort of intelligence might be fascinated with mazes or jigsaw puzzles, or spend available time drawing or wandering off in fantasy land.

Picture Smart people see color and themes and may doodle a considerable measure.

They may express themselves in artistic mediums instead of solely in words. They may think better when they are drawing out their thoughts and feelings.

They might be artists, sculptors, painters, illustrators, computer animators, art teachers, graphic artists, photographers, movie producers, or any sort of designer (interior, landscape, fashion and so forth.).

Programs Ideas

- Incorporate three dimensional objects into your programs. For instance, for Book Trek I acquire instruments and regalia from each of the countries on the off chance that I can
- Tell a Kamishibai story
- Tell a story with puppets, costumes, or flannels
- Tell a string story, a draw and recount story, a cut and recount story
- Incorporate movies into your programs. Weston Woods has

extraordinary open performance movies.

- For Animal Adventures, you can print out pictures of various animals for the kids to take a gander at. For Book trek you can print out pictures from that nation, the banner, and other nation symbols for kids to take a gander at
- Incorporate books that have illustrations or comic books into a program
- Do a program on drawing Anime or Manga or whatever other sort of art like appear, scratch board, water color and so on.
- Do visual games like table games or card games in a program
- Use charts, graphs, maps and so on to illustrate information in a program
- Include open finished crafts in your programs

9. Existential Intelligence or spiritual intelligence

I would characterize existential intelligence as the capacity to be sensitive to, or have the limit with respect to, conceptualizing or handling further or bigger questions about human existence. In my mind folks who have this intelligence are not reluctant to handle considering questions that rotate around such issues as the importance of life, or examine questions like why are we born, why do we die, what is consciousness, or how could we have been able to we arrive?

There are numerous people who feel that there should be a ninth intelligence, existential intelligence (A.K.A.: "wondering smart, cosmic smart, spiritually smart, or metaphysical intelligence"). The possibility of this intelligence has been insinuated by Howard Gardner in several of his works. He has stated that existential intelligence may be manifest in someone who is worried with fundamental questions about existence, or who questions the intricacies of existence. Keeping in mind Professor Gardner has offered a preparatory definition as:

"Individuals who display the proclivity to pose and contemplate questions about life, death, and extreme realities," he has not completely affirmed, endorsed, or described this intelligence.

Perhaps the trouble is that Gardner wisely believes that in the event that he offered an official definition it would open a jar of worms' best let alone for the field of instruction. Or, since a lot of the importance and believability of Gardner's work rests on neurological proof of site specific locations inside the mind, it may be that it is somewhat risky for any author or scientist to conclusively pinpoint the correct biological seat of spiritual ponder or cosmic awareness without culpable any number of people, or some social or religious groups. I think recall that part of the force of Gardner's work depends upon cautious examination of the accessible information and scientific proof. So, right now, it may be safer to say that existential intelligence is the "half" in 8-1/2 intelligences that comprise MI Theory.

Despite this shirking on Gardner's part to absolutely focus on existential intelligence, there are numerous who have acknowledged the presence of this intelligence as reality and have endeavored to clear up what it may look like on the off chance that it were part of the MI exhibit. For those who have met youngsters who seem to have "old souls," it is regularly easy to acknowledge the existence of existential intelligence as something genuine and important. These are the kids who seem to have a sixth sense, they might be exceptionally natural and insightful, even what some may describe as psychic, or they are the ones who pose, and sometimes significantly answer, life's bigger questions like;

- o Why am I here? What are we doing here?
- o Are there different dimensions and if so how are they?
- o Can animals understand us, or do animals go to paradise?
- o Are there truly ghosts?

- Where do we go when we die?
- Why are some people evils?
- Is there life on different planets?
- Where is paradise?
- Where does God live?

These might be those youngsters who can be described as "completely mindful" of the cosmos of its diversity, multifaceted nature, interconnected threads, and its ponder.

Every now and again, these are the kids who persist in asking those "enormous" questions that adults can't or won't answer.

Printed in Great Britain
by Amazon